DINOSAURS

Teacher Created Materials, Inc.
P.O. Box 1040
Huntington Beach, CA 92647
©1986 Teacher Created Materials, Inc.
Made in U.S.A.

ISBN 1-55734-218-0

TABLE OF CONTENTS

The following animals are in chronological order
as they appeared on earth:

Prehistoric Mammals:

DINOSAURS

Millions of years ago, reptiles ruled the earth. Some of these reptiles we call Dinosaurs. Their name means terrible lizard in Latin. Not all dinosaurs were big and terrible. While some were fierce meat eaters, others were peaceful plant eaters. Some dinosaurs were bigger than a schoolbus, but others were smaller than a chicken.

WHERE DID DINOSAURS COME FROM?

1. Some fish called lung fish had strong fins which could move them over the mud from one pond to the next. They had lungs and could survive for a time on land.

2. Early amphibians developed from these fish. They began their lives in the water, and became air-breathing adults. Frogs and toads are amphibians. They must lay their eggs in the water.

3. As the earth changed and became drier, these reptiles developed eggs with tough leathery shells. The newly hatched young could breathe air. Now these reptiles could go wherever they wished.

4. After millions of years, reptiles lived everywhere on our planet. Some developed into the special reptiles we call dinosaurs.

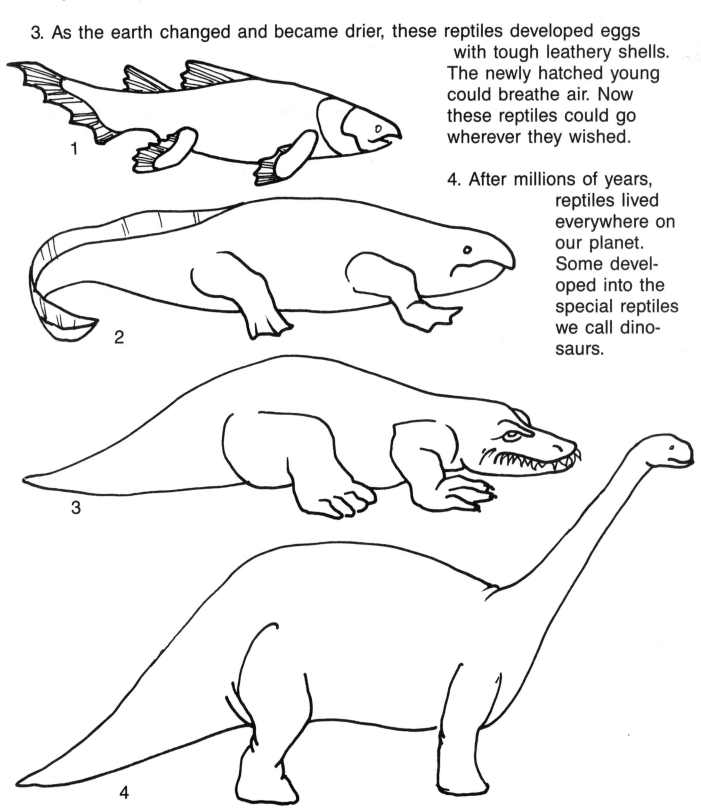

4

FOSSIL PUZZLE

Most of what scientists know about dinosaurs has been learned from fossils. A fossil is the remains of plant or animal life which has been preserved in stone. Scientists try to put together a skeleton to see how the dinosaur looked, what it ate, and how big it was. They can't tell what color it was or if it could growl or whistle. Many times scientists guess what a dinosaur was like by looking at the habits of living animals.

DIRECTIONS:

Draw a 7½'' x 10'' frame on a piece of construction paper. Arrange and glue puzzle pieces from pages 5 and 6 inside the frame.

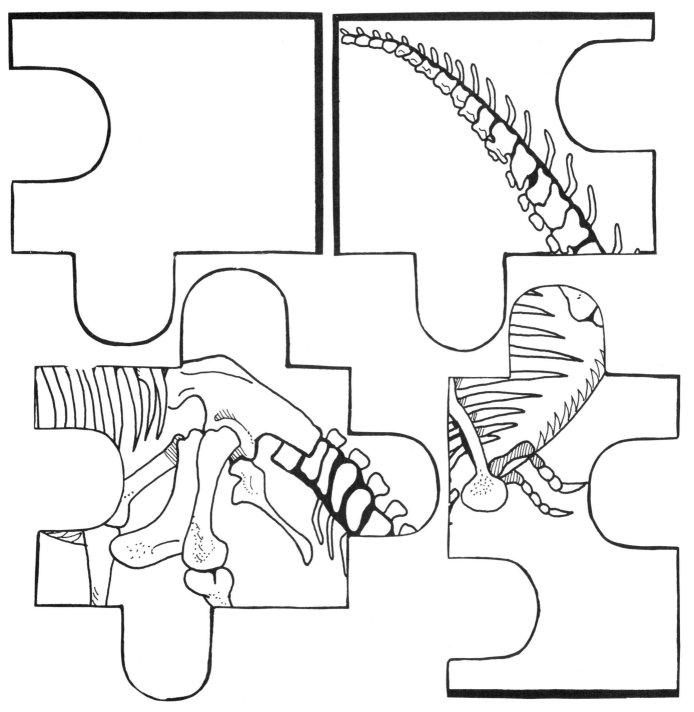

FOSSIL PUZZLE

6

HOW A FOSSIL IS FORMED

1. A dinosaur wades into a river to drink.

2. The dinosaur dies near the river bank.

3. The bones remain there, covered by water and earth.

4. Time passes. The river washes away some bones and buries others.

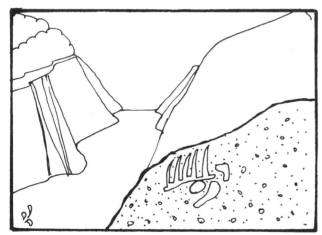

5. After thousands of years, the river has changed its course, leaving the river bank high above the water.

6. Wind and rain move soil away, showing the bones. Now we can discover them.

MAKE A FOSSIL

Some fossils are actual bones or teeth of dinosaurs. Others are prints, such as foot prints of dinosaurs, or impressions left by plants. Still others are called casts, which are spaces left in the stone after the object has decayed away.

TO MAKE A FOSSIL-TYPE PRINT, YOU WILL NEED:

A collection of small bones, leaves, shells, buttons or coins, and a piece of modeling clay the size of your fist.

DIRECTIONS:

1. Press one half of the clay flat and smooth.

2. Place the bone and leaf or other items you have collected onto the clay. Make a few impressions in the clay with a button or coin or twig.

3. Roll out the other half of the clay and place it over the objects on the first half. Press the clay together carefully. When you carefully separate the pieces of clay, you will see prints of the leaves, and a cast of the bone.

8

IS IT A DINOSAUR?

All dinosaurs were reptiles, but not all reptiles were dinosaurs. Dinosaurs were a special kind of reptile. They lived between 200 million and 64 million years ago. They had long tails. Their legs lifted their bodies high off the ground. They were all land animals.

| MOST LIVING REPTILES | CROCODILES & ALLIGATORS | DINOSAURS MAMMALS & BIRDS |

1. Most living reptiles such as lizards and snakes have sprawling postures. Their bodies drag on the ground.

2. Crocodiles and alligators hold their bodies off the ground, but their legs are still out to the side. They cannot run fast for long distances. Their legs cannot support a really large animal.

3. Dinosaurs, mammals and birds have legs tucked up under their bodies. These legs can take large steps and are good for running. They can support a very large animal.

DINOSAUR HIPS

Dinosaurs had special hip bones that allowed their legs to tuck up under their bodies like a mammal's legs, instead of sprawling out to the side like other reptiles. This allowed them to run on two legs, and to keep their bodies off the ground.

The two types of hip bones are called reptile hip and bird hip. Reptile hip dinosaurs include both meat eaters and plant eaters. Bird hip dinosaurs were all vegetarian.

QUESTIONS:

Were all dinosaurs reptiles?
Were all reptiles dinosaurs?
What did bird hip dinosaurs eat?
What did reptile hip dinosaurs eat?

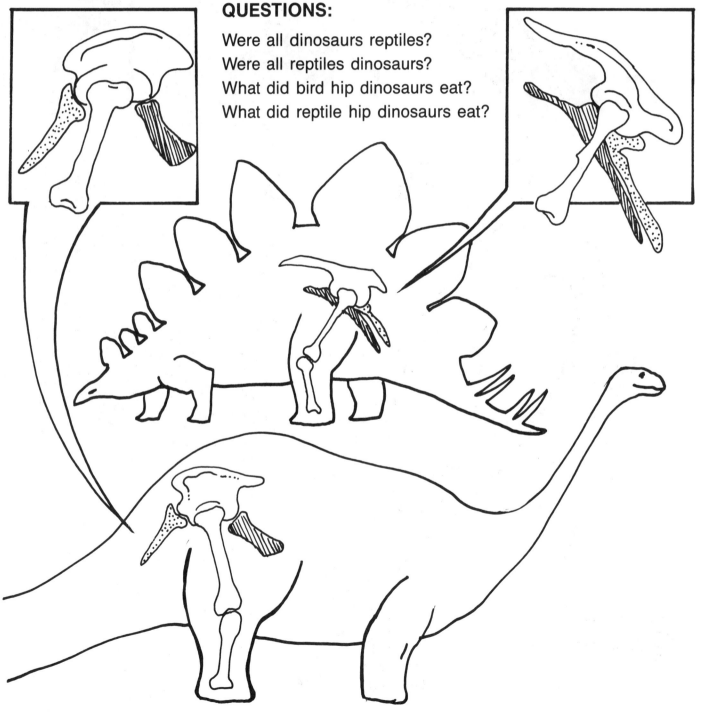

COELOPHYSIS
(SEE-loh-FY-ses)

Coelophysis made its first appearance about 180 million years ago. It is one of the earliest dinosaurs. Its skeleton shows us that it was a fast runner, moving on its hind legs and holding its long tail off the ground. It was about three feet high and eight feet long. It ate insects, frogs and lizards, maybe even eggs from other dinosaurs.

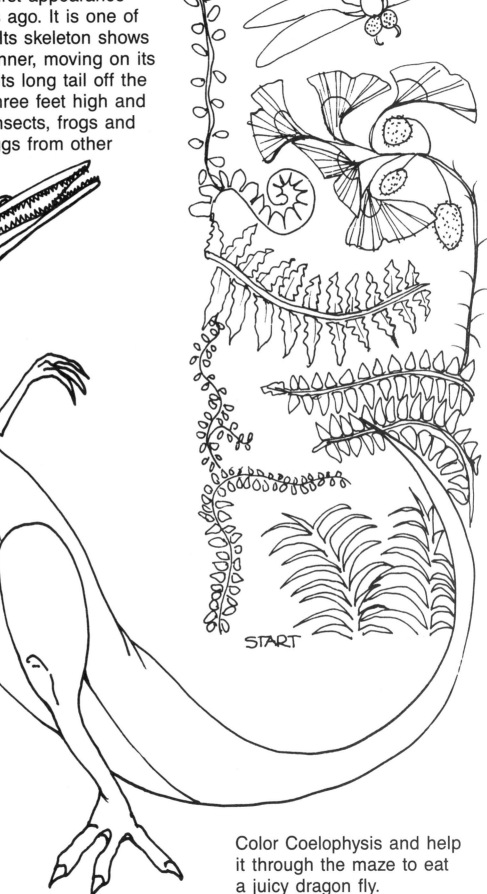

START

Color Coelophysis and help it through the maze to eat a juicy dragon fly.

#218 Dinosaurs

DIMETRODON
(di-ME-troh-dawn)

Dimetrodon is not a dinosaur. It is a very early reptile with mammal-like teeth. It is a meat eater. Scientists think Dimetrodon used its big sail to control its body temperature. Dimetrodon could let the sun shine on the sail to get warm quickly. In a cool or shady place the sail would help Dimetrodon cool off.

Scientists know that Dimetrodon is not a dinosaur by looking at its teeth. Can you tell another reason why Dimetrodon is not a dinosaur?

ANSWER:

The legs of Dimetrodon are sprawled out to the side of its body like a reptile, not tucked up under its body like a mammal's legs. If they did, the body would drag on the ground.

ALLOSAURUS
(Al-uh-SAW-ruhs)

Allosaurus was a fierce hunter. It had three fingered claws on the end of each arm, with talons as sharp as razors. Its mouth was crowded with sharp teeth three inches long! It was 34 feet long and 10 feet high. Its favorite food was other dinosaurs, especially the huge apatosaurus. It probably hunted together with other Allosaurus when hunting for large beasts.

Circle the Allosaurus' favorite food.

APATOSAURUS
(uh-PAT-uh-SAW-ruhs)

One of the best known dinosaurs is one many people call Brontosaurus. Scientists call it Apatosaurus. It was the biggest animal to live on land. From the tip of its nose to the tip of its tail, Apatosaurus was eighty feet long. It stood 15 feet high at the shoulder and weighed as much as five elephants. Apatosaurus lived to be over 200 years old. Apatosaurus was a peaceful giant who spent its time looking for the most tender swamp plants.

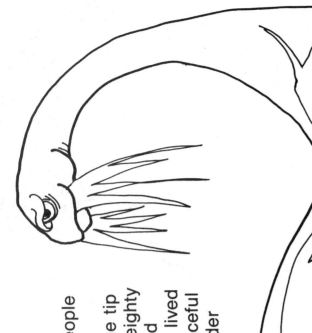

ARCHEOPTERYX
(AHR-kee-AHP-tuh-riks)

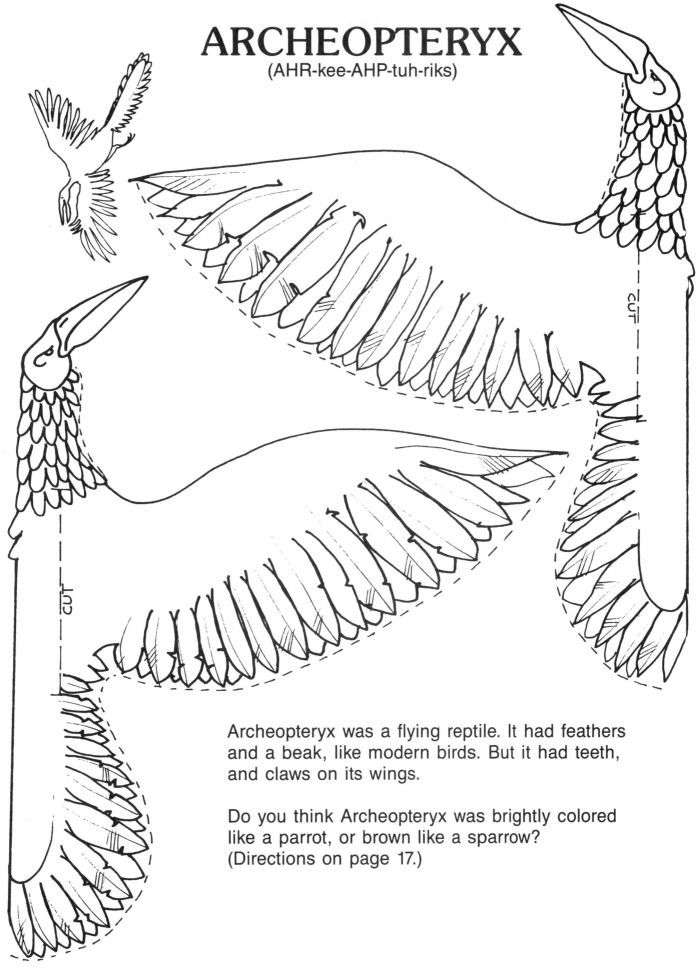

Archeopteryx was a flying reptile. It had feathers and a beak, like modern birds. But it had teeth, and claws on its wings.

Do you think Archeopteryx was brightly colored like a parrot, or brown like a sparrow? (Directions on page 17.)

PTERANODON
(tare-AN-oh-DON)

The Pteranodon is not a dinosaur. It is a
flying reptile which lived at the same time
as many dinosaurs. Pteranodon had wings
of skin which it used like a sail. Pteranodon
could climb up a tree and glide down to the
ground or to another tree. It could not fly by
flapping its wings as modern birds do.
Pteranodon had a long curved jaw full of
very sharp teeth. It had claws on its wings.
Scientists think that Pteranodon slept
upside down, just like modern bats do.

(Directions on page 17.)

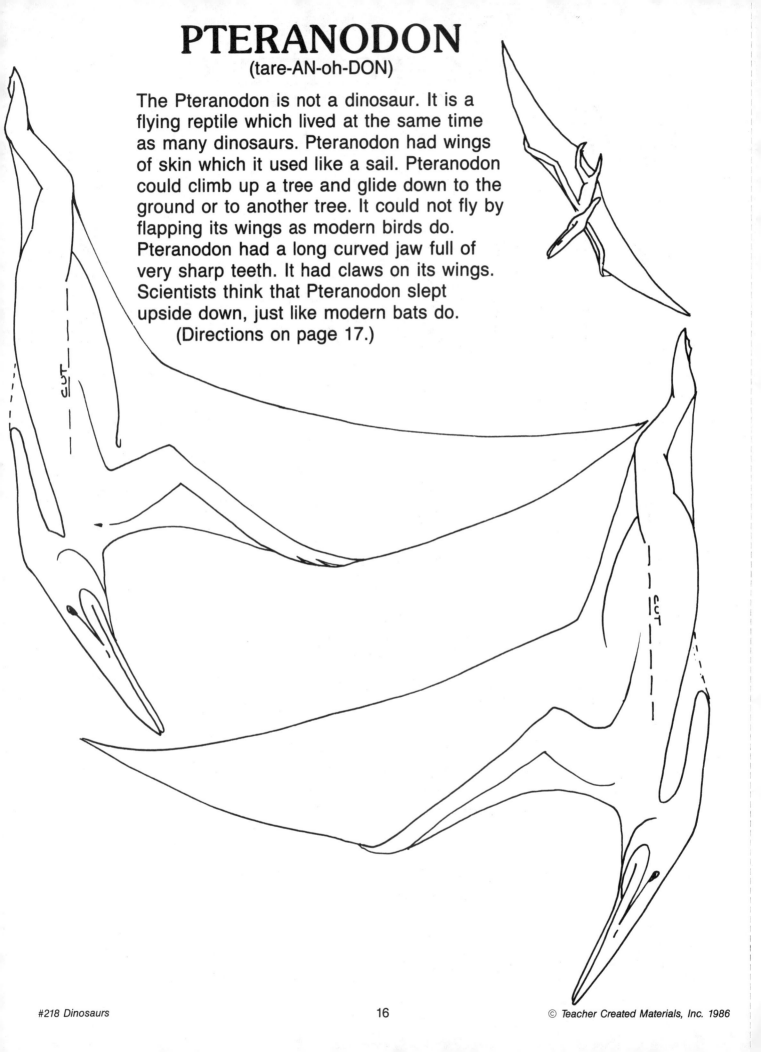

HOW TO MAKE A FLYING REPTILE

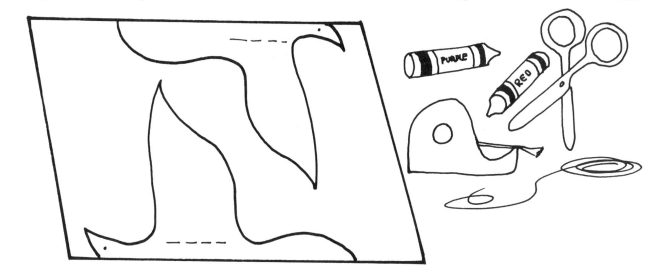

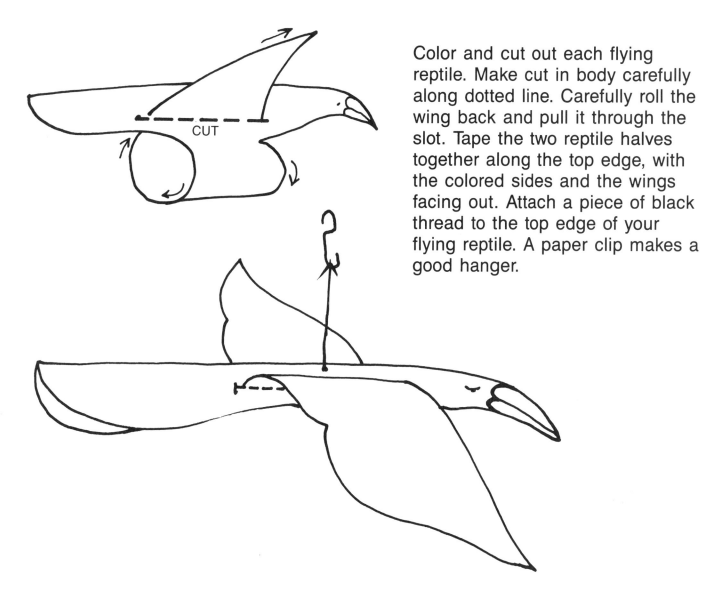

Color and cut out each flying reptile. Make cut in body carefully along dotted line. Carefully roll the wing back and pull it through the slot. Tape the two reptile halves together along the top edge, with the colored sides and the wings facing out. Attach a piece of black thread to the top edge of your flying reptile. A paper clip makes a good hanger.

#218 Dinosaurs

STEGOSAURUS
(STEG-uh-SAW-ruhs)

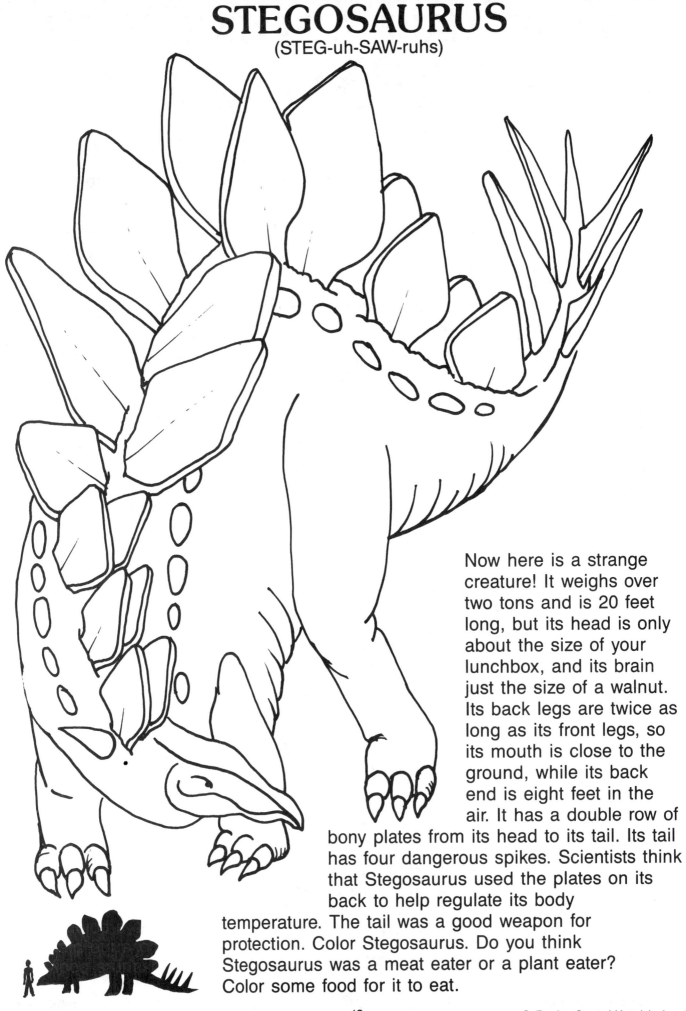

Now here is a strange creature! It weighs over two tons and is 20 feet long, but its head is only about the size of your lunchbox, and its brain just the size of a walnut. Its back legs are twice as long as its front legs, so its mouth is close to the ground, while its back end is eight feet in the air. It has a double row of bony plates from its head to its tail. Its tail has four dangerous spikes. Scientists think that Stegosaurus used the plates on its back to help regulate its body temperature. The tail was a good weapon for protection. Color Stegosaurus. Do you think Stegosaurus was a meat eater or a plant eater? Color some food for it to eat.

18

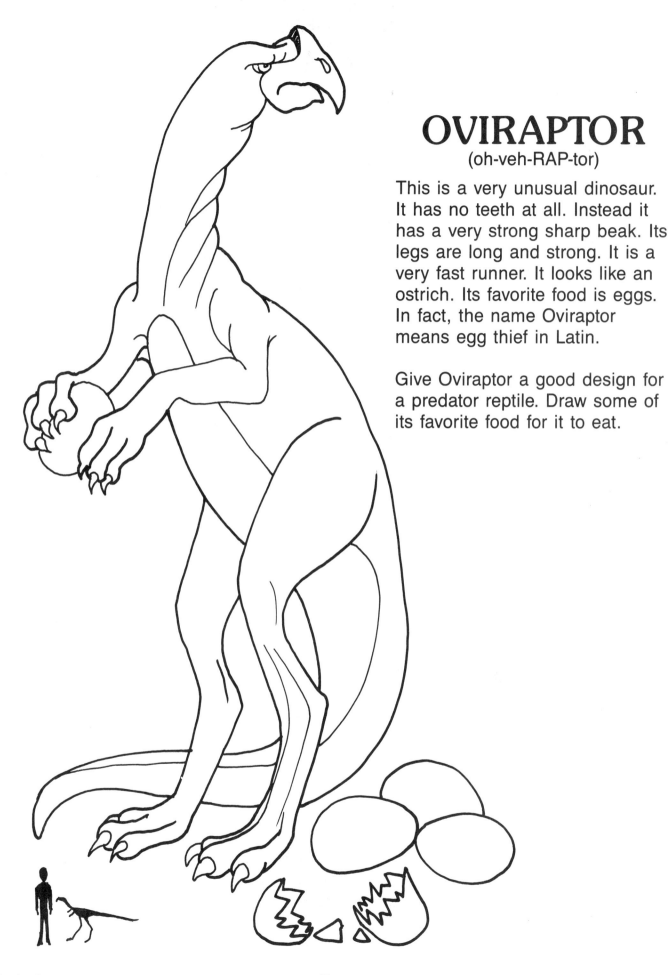

OVIRAPTOR
(oh-veh-RAP-tor)

This is a very unusual dinosaur. It has no teeth at all. Instead it has a very strong sharp beak. Its legs are long and strong. It is a very fast runner. It looks like an ostrich. Its favorite food is eggs. In fact, the name Oviraptor means egg thief in Latin.

Give Oviraptor a good design for a predator reptile. Draw some of its favorite food for it to eat.

ELASMOSAURUS
(eh-LAS-muh-SAW-ruhs)
ICTHYOSAURUS
(ick-thee-uh-SAW-ruhs)

ELASMOSAURUS

ICTHYOSAURUS

Elasmosaurus and Icthyosaurus are marine reptiles. They are air breathing animals which live in the water, and do not come onto the land. They are not dinosaurs. Can you tell why?

Color Elasmosaurus and Icthyosaurus. Give them good colors for sea-going creatures. Draw some food for them to eat.

ANATOSAURUS
(uh-NAT-uh-SAW-ruhs)

Anatosaurus can be found in wet and swampy areas. Its favorite food is the plants it finds there. It can gather large mouthfuls in its huge duck-bill. It has many strong teeth for chewing the tough leaves and stems. Anatosaurus is a very good swimmer and can hide in the swamp from its enemies.

Color Anatosaurus. Draw some food for it to eat.

ANKYLOSAURUS
(ANG-kih-loh-SAW-ruhs)

Here is another animal who doesn't want to be eaten. Its body is covered with thick bony plates. Along its sides are sharp horns. Its tail is very dangerous, with a heavy bony knob on the end. Ankylosaurus can swing its tail like a big club. If a predator comes by, Ankylosaurus can crouch down under its shell. But here, Tyrannosaurus wouldn't go away. Ankylosaurus is giving him a whack on the leg. Very painful!

WHAM!

ANKYLOSAURUS

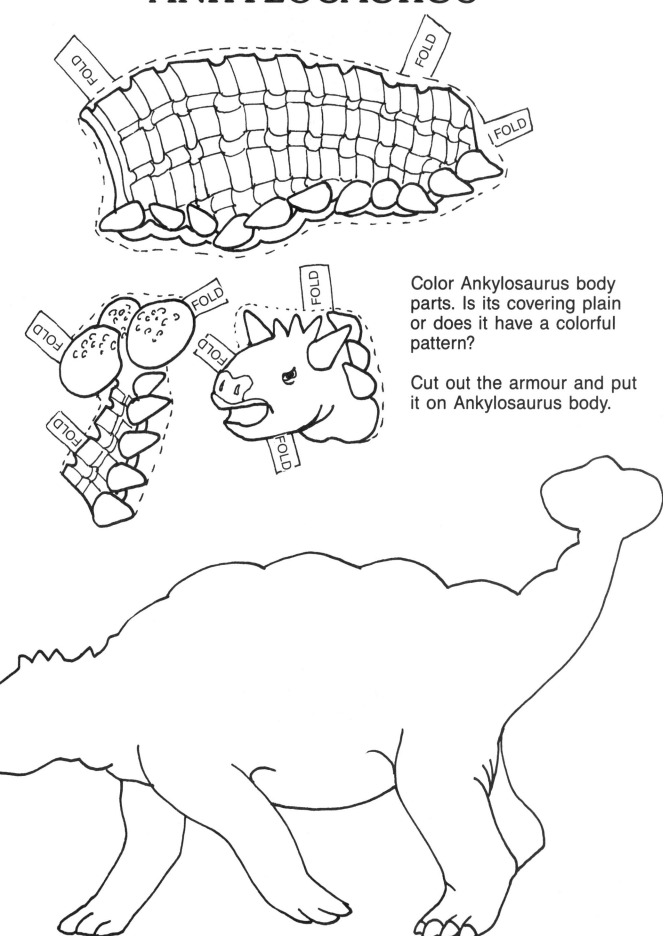

Color Ankylosaurus body parts. Is its covering plain or does it have a colorful pattern?

Cut out the armour and put it on Ankylosaurus body.

PROTOCERATOPS
(PROH-doh-SERR-uh-tahps)

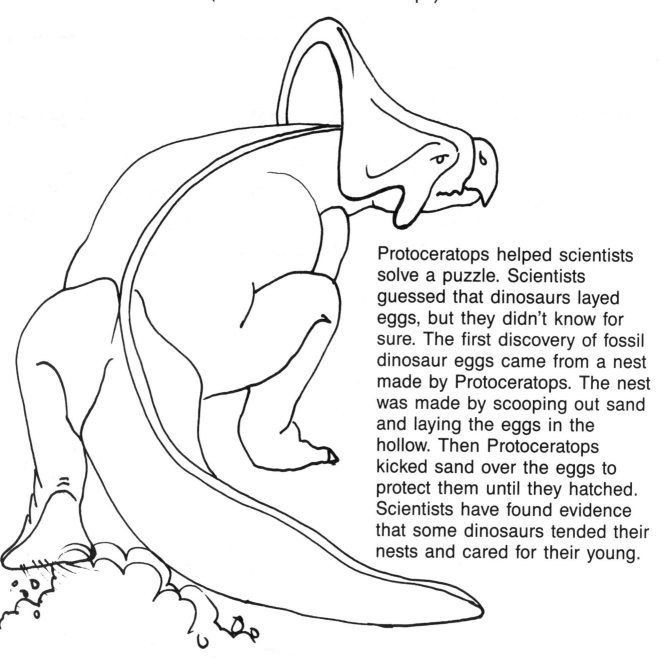

Protoceratops helped scientists solve a puzzle. Scientists guessed that dinosaurs layed eggs, but they didn't know for sure. The first discovery of fossil dinosaur eggs came from a nest made by Protoceratops. The nest was made by scooping out sand and laying the eggs in the hollow. Then Protoceratops kicked sand over the eggs to protect them until they hatched. Scientists have found evidence that some dinosaurs tended their nests and cared for their young.

CUT
├ - - - - - ┤

PROTOCERATOPS

Color Protoceratops. Color the nest and eggs and baby Protoceratops. Make a small cut on page 24 where shown. Cut out all of the pieces. Put the tab of baby Protoceratops through the small cut you have made. Glue the nest and eggs into place. Leave room for baby Protoceratops to pop up out of his nest.

PUSH →

COUNT THE EGGS

Baby Dino has just hatched. Count the eggs to see how many brothers and sisters he will have.

PACHYCEPHALOSAURUS
(PAK-ee-SEF-al-uh-SAW-ruhs)

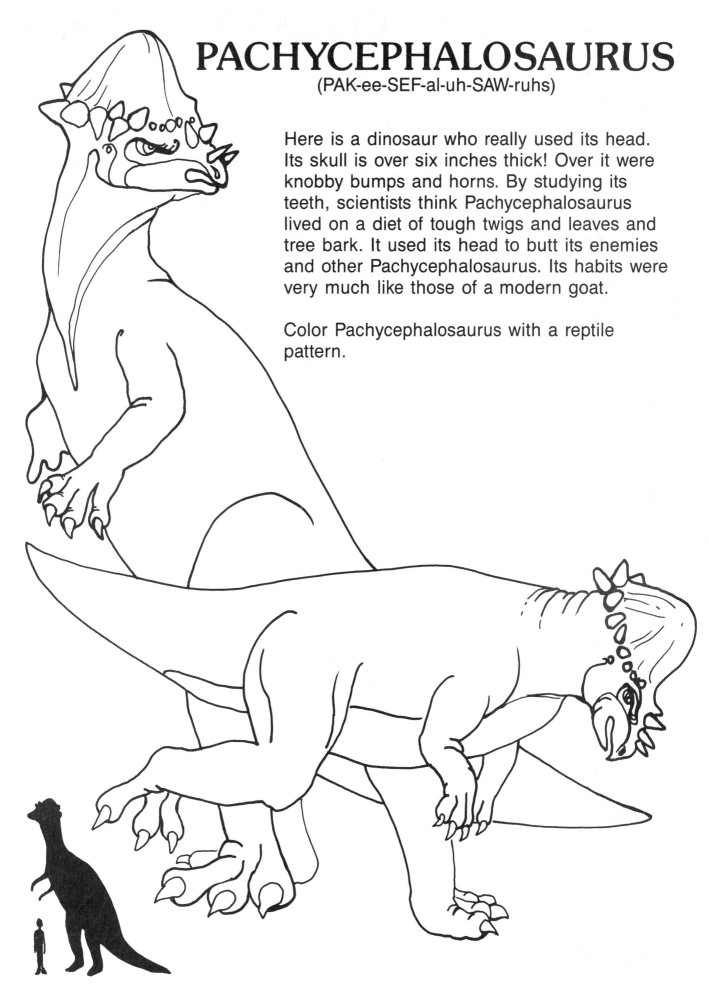

Here is a dinosaur who really used its head. Its skull is over six inches thick! Over it were knobby bumps and horns. By studying its teeth, scientists think Pachycephalosaurus lived on a diet of tough twigs and leaves and tree bark. It used its head to butt its enemies and other Pachycephalosaurus. Its habits were very much like those of a modern goat.

Color Pachycephalosaurus with a reptile pattern.

PARASAUROLOPHOUS

(par-uh-sawr-AHL-uh-fuhs)

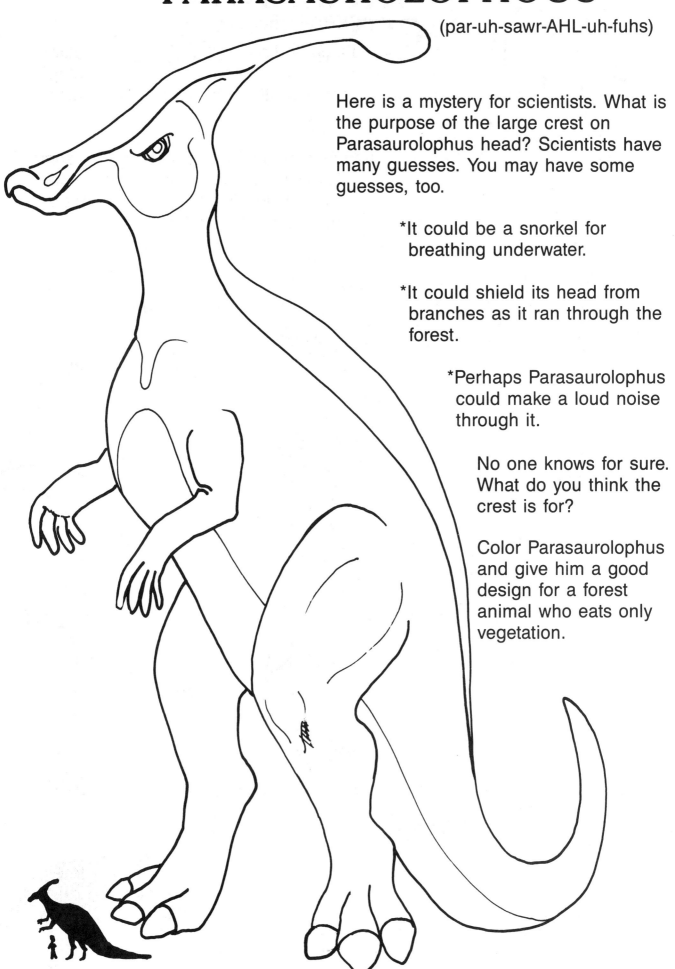

Here is a mystery for scientists. What is the purpose of the large crest on Parasaurolophus head? Scientists have many guesses. You may have some guesses, too.

*It could be a snorkel for breathing underwater.

*It could shield its head from branches as it ran through the forest.

*Perhaps Parasaurolophus could make a loud noise through it.

No one knows for sure. What do you think the crest is for?

Color Parasaurolophus and give him a good design for a forest animal who eats only vegetation.

TRICERATOPS
(try-SERR-uh-tahps)

Triceratops means 'three horned face' in Latin. Although a plant eater, Triceratops horns were not for show. It was a fierce fighter! Triceratops fought with each other. They fought with other dinosaurs who wanted to eat them.

Triceratops lived in herds. Here, some Triceratops face an enemy. Why were the smaller Triceratops kept in the middle of the herd?

TYRANNOSAURUS REX
(tie-RAHN-uhSAW-ruhs-REX)

Tyrannosaurus Rex was the biggest flesh-eating animal ever to live on our planet. Standing on its huge hind legs, it was taller than a house. A grown man would reach only up to its knee. Its body was 7½ tons of muscle, bones, and teeth.

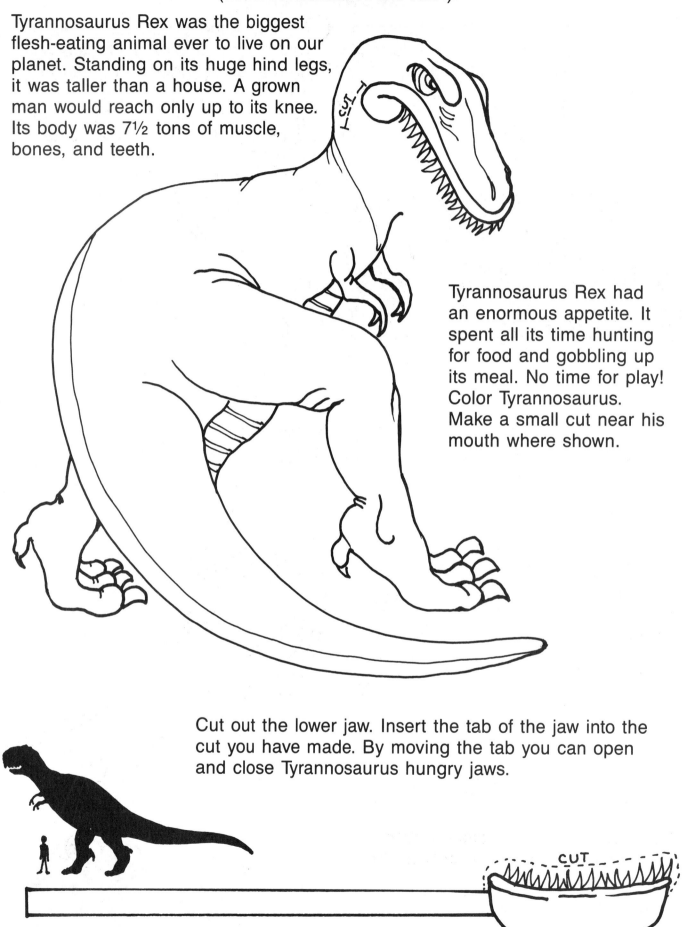

Tyrannosaurus Rex had an enormous appetite. It spent all its time hunting for food and gobbling up its meal. No time for play! Color Tyrannosaurus. Make a small cut near his mouth where shown.

Cut out the lower jaw. Insert the tab of the jaw into the cut you have made. By moving the tab you can open and close Tyrannosaurus hungry jaws.

CUT

30

DINOSAUR PENCIL TOPPERS

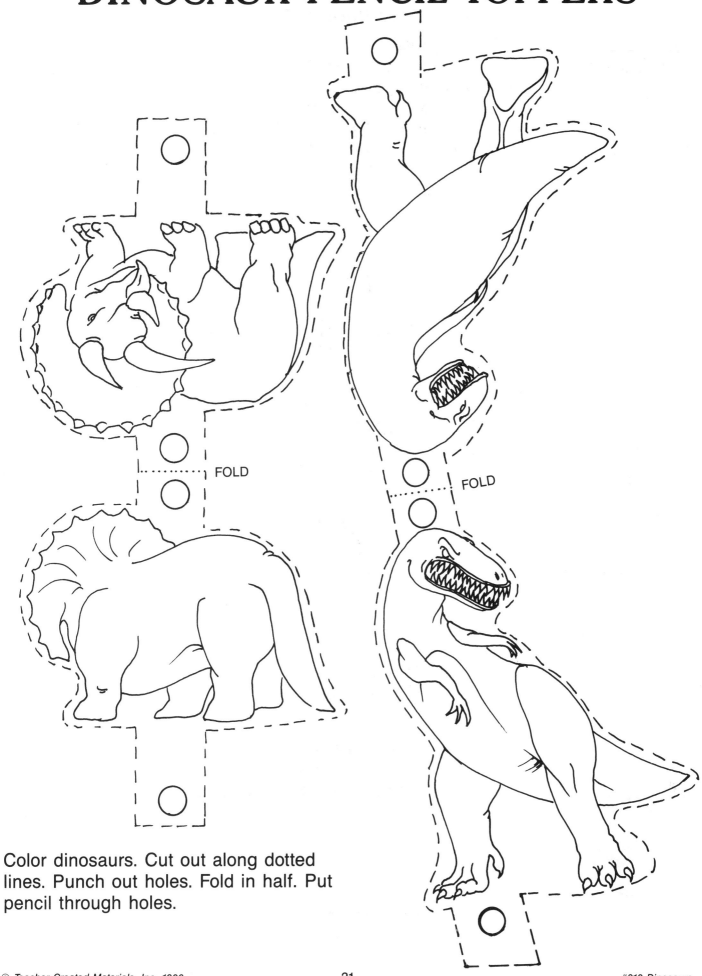

FOLD

FOLD

Color dinosaurs. Cut out along dotted lines. Punch out holes. Fold in half. Put pencil through holes.

DINOSAUR WEAPONS

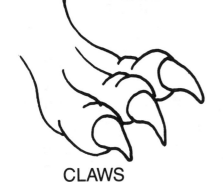

CLAWS

HORNS

TEETH

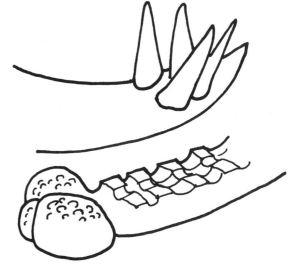

TAIL SPIKES & CLUBS

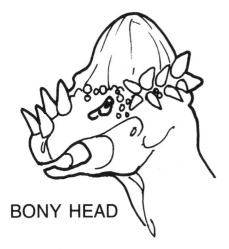

BONY HEAD

Name some other dinosaur weapons.

_____

_____

_____

TYRO GAME

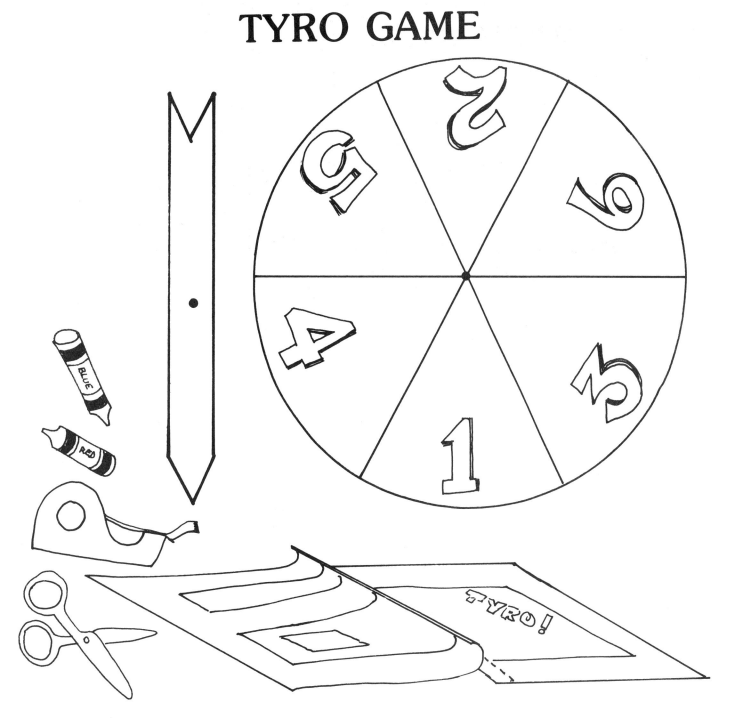

Color gameboard squares. Color arrow and numbered circle. Color and cut out tyro cards. Trim the edges of gameboard along dotted line. Attach to gameboard B with tape. Make the dotted lines of A and B touch. Use buttons for gameboard markers.

TO PLAY:
Players put their markers on "START." Each player spins for a number. The highest number goes first. At the beginning of your turn, spin the spinner and move your marker the number of spaces shown. If your marker lands on "TYRO" choose a tyro card and follow the directions. Return the card to the bottom of the stack. The first player to reach "SAFE" wins.

34

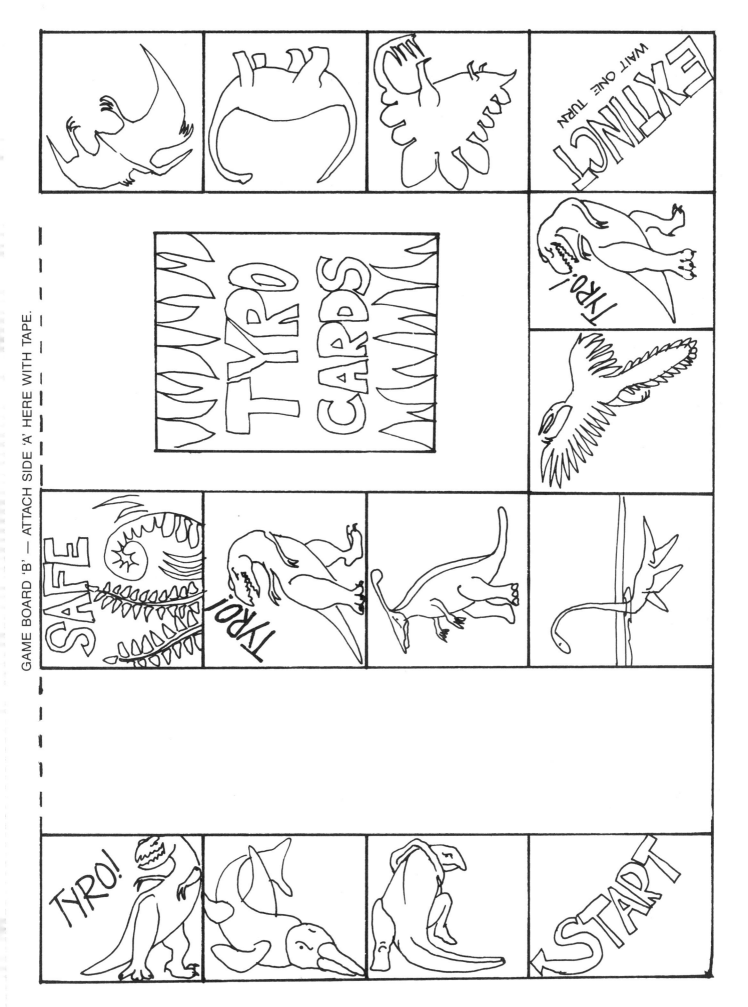

#218 Dinosaurs

YOU DIVE INTO A SWAMP TO ESCAPE FROM TYRO. SKIP 1 TURN.

YOU ARE INJURED BY TYRO. GO BACK 1 SPACE.

TYRO STEPS ON YOUR TOE. SKIP 1 TURN.

TYRO FINDS YOUR FOOD SUPPLY. IT MAKES HIM SICK. MOVE AHEAD 1 SPACE.

TYRO CHASES YOU INTO QUICKSAND. GO BACK 2 SPACES.

TYRO CATCHES YOU SLEEPING. MOVE BACK 2 SPACES.

YOU CATCH TYRO SLEEPING. MOVE AHEAD 2 SPACES (*VERY* QUIETLY).

TYRO STAMPEDES A HERD OF TRICERATOPS. MOVE AHEAD 1 SPACE.

YOU HIDE FROM TYRO BEHIND A FERN. YOUR CAMOFLAGE SAVES YOU. MOVE AHEAD 1 SPACE.

TYRO CHASES YOU UP A TREE. SKIP 1 TURN.

YOU HIDE BEHIND A ROCK. TYRO SEES YOU! MOVE BACK 1 SPACE.

TYRO CATCHES YOU IN HIS JAWS. YOU ESCAPE. SKIP 1 TURN.

36

NOT ALL DINOSAURS LIVED AT THE SAME TIME

200 MILLION YEARS AGO

COELOPHYSIS
DIMETRODON

160 MILLION YEARS AGO

ALLOSAURUS
APATOSAURUS
ARCHEOPTERYX
ORNITHOLESTES
STEGOSAURUS

150 MILLION YEARS AGO

ELASMOSAURUS
ICTHYOSAURUS

135 MILLION YEARS AGO

PTERODON

100 MILLION YEARS AGO

ANATOSAURUS
ANKYLOSAURUS
PACHYCEPHALASAURUS
PARASAUROLOPHUS
PROTOCERATOPS
TRICERATOPS
TYRANNOSAURUS

THEORIES OF EXTINCTION

About 64 million years ago, dinosaurs suddenly became extinct. Scientists have many theories about what happened to the dinosaurs, but the answer is still a mystery.

1. Egg-eating mammals ate all the dinosaur eggs.

2. The continents did not always appear as they do on maps today. Long ago the continents began to slowly drift closer together. This caused the shallow areas where sea creatures lived to disappear. It also caused the weather to change. Now the land animals and the sea animals could not find food or good places to live.

3. In a nearby constellation a star exploded, creating a super-nova which bathed the earth in deadly cosmic rays. Smaller reptiles and early mammals survived. The large dinosaurs died.

4. A meteorite storm bombarded the earth with millions of meteorites. As they crashed into the earth and into the sea, huge clouds of dust and steam covered the earth and blocked out the sun's rays for many years. The earth's temperature became very cold in just a short time. The dinosaurs and the jungle-like plants could not survive in the cold and dark. As the earth began to cool, huge sheets of ice formed at the earth's poles. This was the beginning of the ice age. Big rivers of ice, called glaciers moved into the once warm areas of the earth, turning them cold and carving out valleys. Mountain ranges began pushing up as the earth's continents moved together. The animal forms which thrived in this climate were very different from the dinosaurs which thrived in a warm steamy tropical environment. These new animals needed fur to keep warm. They needed to be warmblooded, so that they could regulate their own temperature. They could no longer depend on the sun to keep them warm.

DELTATHERIUM
(dell-tah-THEER-ee-um)

This furry mammal is about the size of a mouse. He has fur. His sharp teeth are good for eating insects. For thousands of years he has been keeping out of Tyrannosaurus' way, but now there is plenty of room for Deltatherium.

Find all the Deltatherium on this page. Color them. Help them hide in the ferns.

DIATRYMA and EOHIPPUS
(DIE-uhTRY-ma)   (ee-uh-HIP-pus)

Diatryma was a huge bird. Its wings were too small for flight. Perhaps it ate only seeds, or perhaps it ate small mammals like Eohippus.

Eohippus means dawn horse. He was only 12 inches tall. He had paws with toes on them to help him run over the marshy ground. It will be millions of years before he looks like horses of today. He eats mostly small plants and leaves. He travels in a herd.

IMPERIAL MAMMOTH

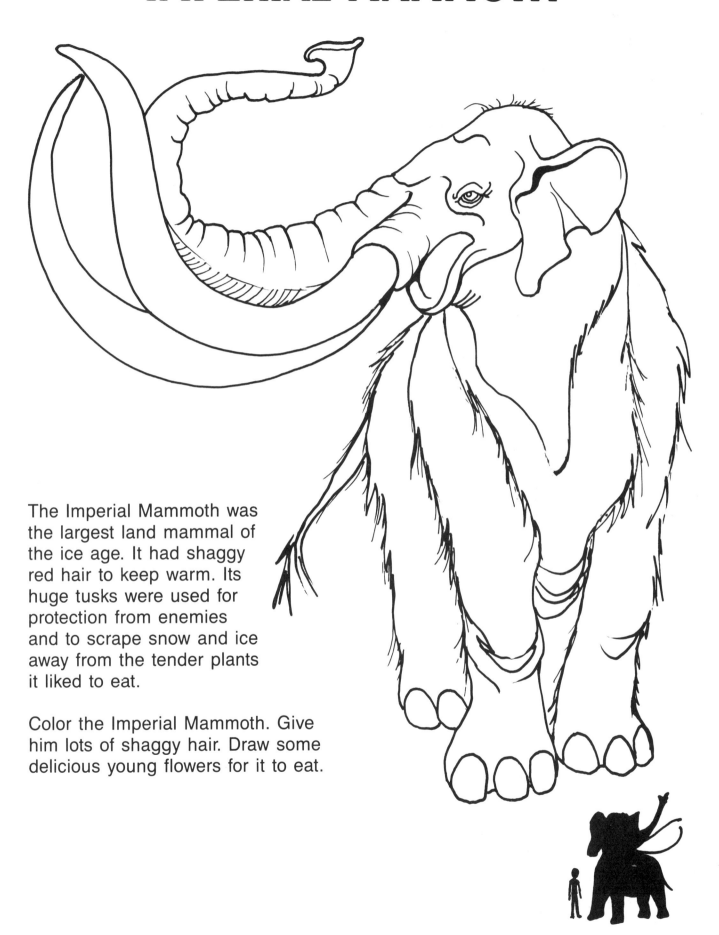

The Imperial Mammoth was the largest land mammal of the ice age. It had shaggy red hair to keep warm. Its huge tusks were used for protection from enemies and to scrape snow and ice away from the tender plants it liked to eat.

Color the Imperial Mammoth. Give him lots of shaggy hair. Draw some delicious young flowers for it to eat.

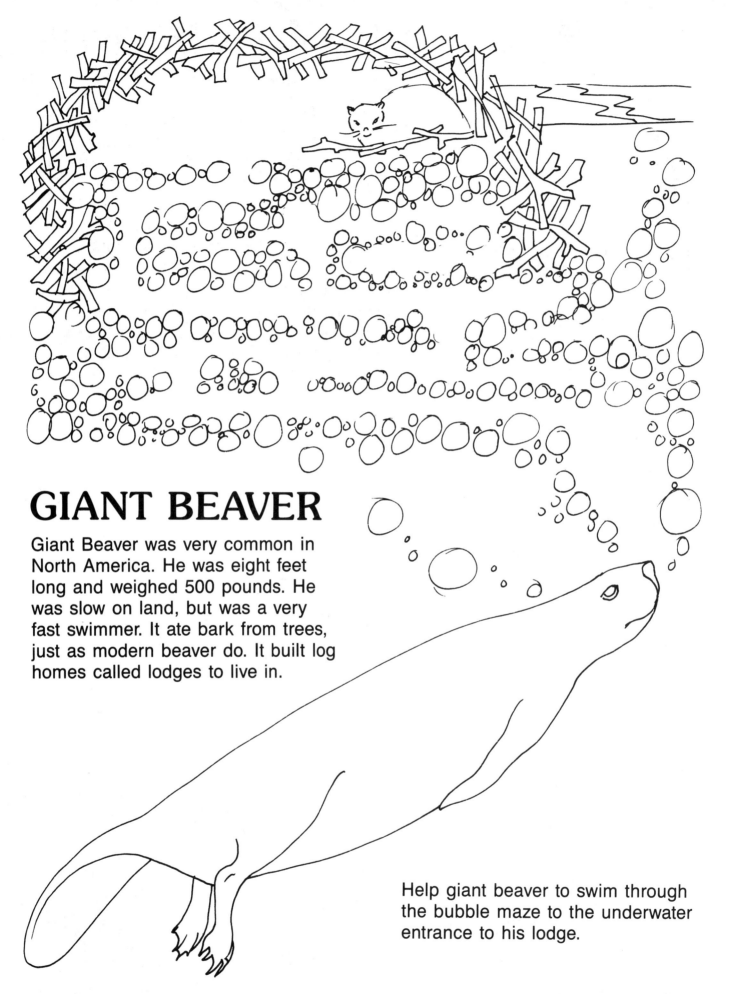

GIANT BEAVER

Giant Beaver was very common in North America. He was eight feet long and weighed 500 pounds. He was slow on land, but was a very fast swimmer. It ate bark from trees, just as modern beaver do. It built log homes called lodges to live in.

Help giant beaver to swim through the bubble maze to the underwater entrance to his lodge.

MOROPUS
(mo-ROW-pus)

Moropus is a curious animal. It had a long neck and its front legs were much longer than its back legs. It had a head like a horse and claws like a cat. His long neck probably helped him to reach leaves and branches. His claws may have been for defense, or maybe to help grasp the branches it used for food. What do you think its claws were for? Color Moropus. Give its coat a good design for a plant eating forest animal.

#218 Dinosaurs

SMILODON
(SMILE-uh-don)

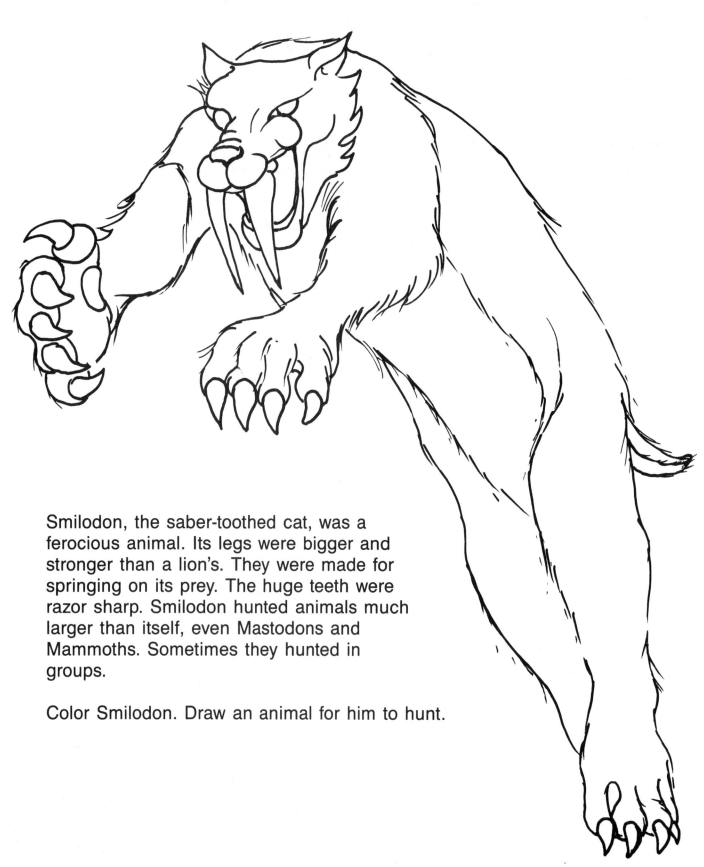

Smilodon, the saber-toothed cat, was a ferocious animal. Its legs were bigger and stronger than a lion's. They were made for springing on its prey. The huge teeth were razor sharp. Smilodon hunted animals much larger than itself, even Mastodons and Mammoths. Sometimes they hunted in groups.

Color Smilodon. Draw an animal for him to hunt.

GLYPTODON
(GLIP-toh-don)

Glyptodon was covered with a hard shell for protection. When a predator came near, it could crouch under its shell until the danger passed. Glyptodon also had a weapon. His tail was covered with bony spikes. He could defend himself.

QUESTIONS:

Which dinosaurs had tails like Glyptodons?

Which dinosaurs had armour like Glyptodons?

Would Glyptodon make a good meal for a saber-toothed cat?

MAMMAL FINGER PUPPETS

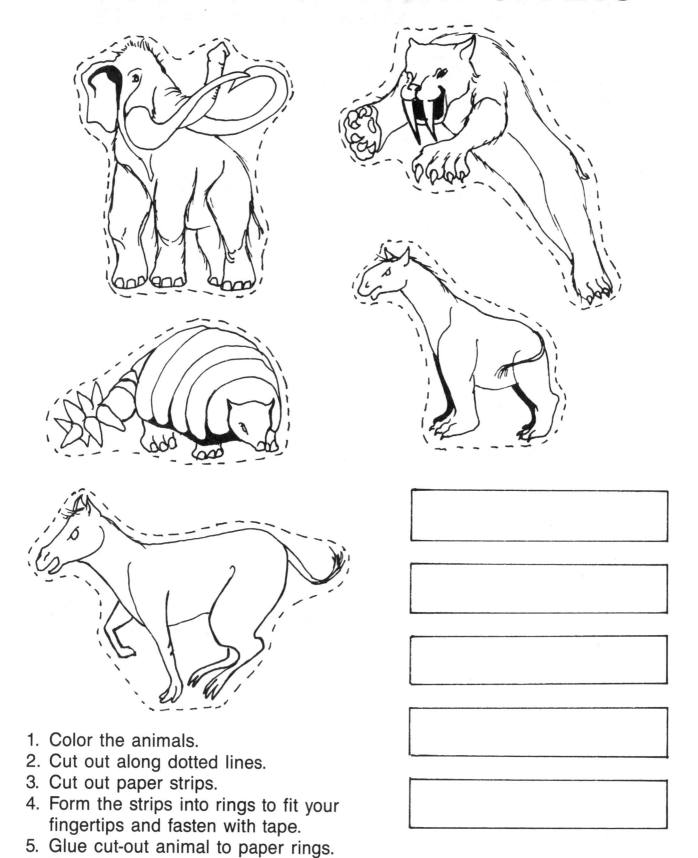

1. Color the animals.
2. Cut out along dotted lines.
3. Cut out paper strips.
4. Form the strips into rings to fit your fingertips and fasten with tape.
5. Glue cut-out animal to paper rings.
6. Have fun!

MAMMAL WORD SEARCH

Find the names of these mammals hidden in the word search.

SMILODON

GLYPTODON

DELTATHERIUM

GIANT BEAVER

MOROPUS

EOHIPPUS

MAMMOTH

D	O	Z	L	C	M	R	Y	A	B	X
E	Y	E	P	S	G	L	N	T	U	R
L	R	S	B	K	L	L	J	I	P	M
T	Y	C	D	F	Y	Q	V	W	T	O
A	E	O	H	I	P	P	U	S	N	R
T	D	T	R	B	T	W	O	R	T	O
H	M	A	M	M	O	T	H	N	A	P
E	O	D	L	A	D	U	L	A	R	U
R	U	C	O	L	O	N	D	B	W	S
I	S	X	T	L	N	T	J	H	K	N
U	E	B	M	B	S	L	B	S	Y	J
M	S	M	I	L	O	D	O	N	I	O
G	I	A	N	T	B	E	A	V	E	R

DINOSAUR ANSWER KEY

GLYPTODON

SMILODON

DELTATHERIUM

GIANT BEAVER

MOROPUS

EOHIPPUS

MAMMOTH

Word search grid:

D	O	Z	L	C	M	R	Y	A	B	X
E	Y	E	P	S	G	L	N	T	U	R
L	R	S	B	K	L	L	J	I	P	M
T	Y	C	D	F	Y	Q	V	W	T	O
A	E	O	H	I	P	P	U	S	N	R
T	D	T	R	B	T	W	O	R	T	O
H	M	A	M	M	O	T	H	N	A	P
E	O	D	L	A	D	U	L	A	R	U
R	U	C	O	L	O	N	D	B	W	S
I	S	X	T	L	N	T	J	H	K	N
U	E	B	M	B	S	L	B	S	Y	J
M	S	M	I	L	O	D	O	N	I	O
G	I	A	N	T	B	E	A	V	E	R